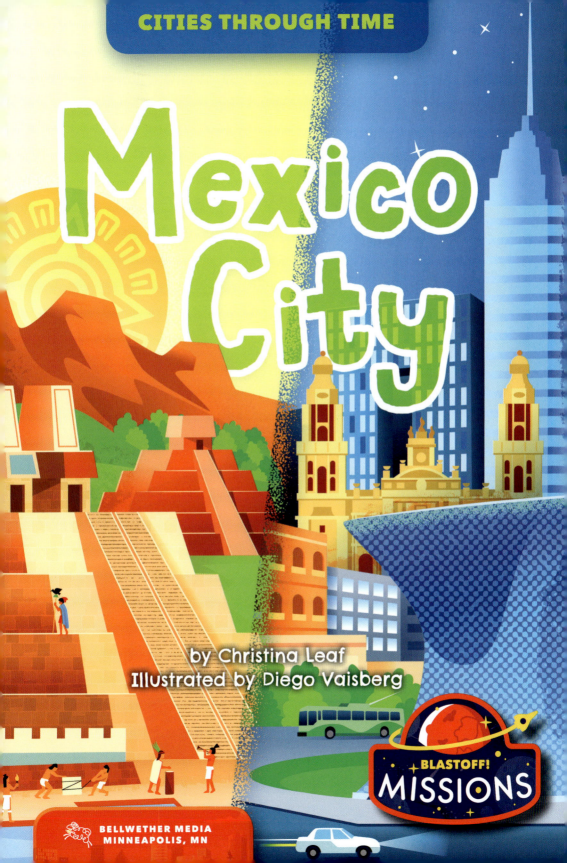

Blastoff! Missions takes you on a learning adventure! Colorful illustrations and exciting narratives highlight cool facts about our world and beyond. Read the mission goals and follow the narrative to gain knowledge, build reading skills, and have fun!

Traditional Nonfiction

Narrative Nonfiction

Blastoff! Universe

MISSION GOALS

> FIND YOUR SIGHT WORDS IN THE BOOK.

> LEARN ABOUT DIFFERENT PERIODS IN MEXICO CITY'S HISTORY.

> LEARN ABOUT DIFFERENT GROUPS OF PEOPLE WHO HAVE LIVED IN MEXICO CITY.

This edition first published in 2024 by Bellwether Media, Inc.

No part of this publication may be reproduced in whole or in part without written permission of the publisher. For information regarding permission, write to Bellwether Media, Inc., Attention: Permissions Department, 6012 Blue Circle Drive, Minnetonka, MN 55343.

Library of Congress Cataloging-in-Publication Data

Names: Leaf, Christina, author. | Vaisberg, Diego, illustrator.
Title: Mexico City / by Christina Leaf ; [illustrated by] Diego Vaisberg.
Description: Minneapolis, MN : Bellwether Media, 2024. | Series: Cities through time | Includes bibliographical references and index. | Audience: Ages 5-8 | Audience: Grades 2-3 | Summary: "Vibrant illustrations accompany information about the history of Mexico City. The narrative nonfiction text is intended for students in kindergarten through third grade." Provided by publisher.
Identifiers: LCCN 2023014276 (print) | LCCN 2023014277 (ebook) | ISBN 9798886873825 (library binding) | ISBN 9798886875201 (paperback) | ISBN 9798886875706 (ebook)
Subjects: LCSH: Mexico City (Mexico)--Juvenile literature.
Classification: LCC F1386 .L43 2024 (print) | LCC F1386 (ebook) | DDC 972/.53--dc23/eng/20230404
LC record available at https://lccn.loc.gov/2023014276
LC ebook record available at https://lccn.loc.gov/2023014277

Text copyright © 2024 by Bellwether Media, Inc. BLASTOFF! MISSIONS and associated logos are trademarks and/or registered trademarks of Bellwether Media, Inc.

Editor: Betsy Rathburn   Designer: Andrea Schneider

Printed in the United States of America, North Mankato, MN.

This is **Blastoff Jimmy**! He is here to help you on your mission and share fun facts along the way!

Table of Contents

Welcome to Mexico City!	4
A Grand Capital	6
A Spanish City	8
Finding Freedom	12
The City Today	18
Glossary	22
To Learn More	23
Beyond the Mission	24
Index	24

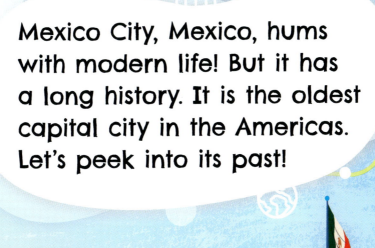

Mexico City, Mexico, hums with modern life! But it has a long history. It is the oldest capital city in the Americas. Let's peek into its past!

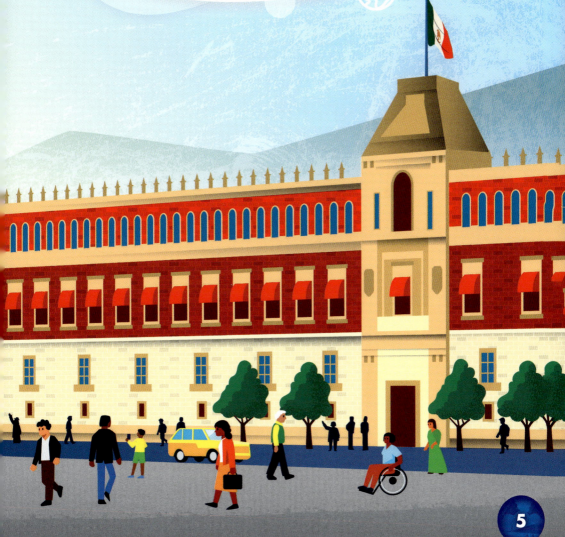

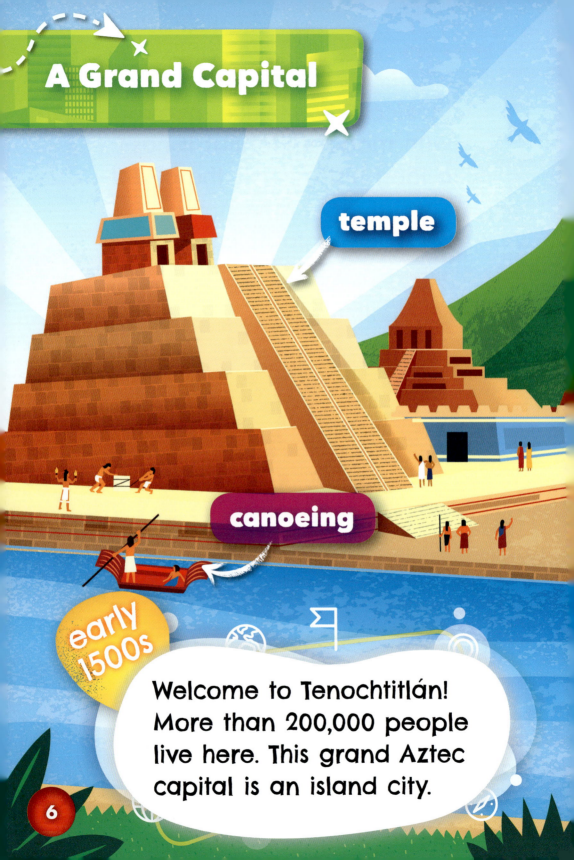

JIMMY SAYS
The city was founded in 1325. Aztecs believed that gods showed them the site.

It sits in the middle of a lake. We can canoe past its many **temples**.

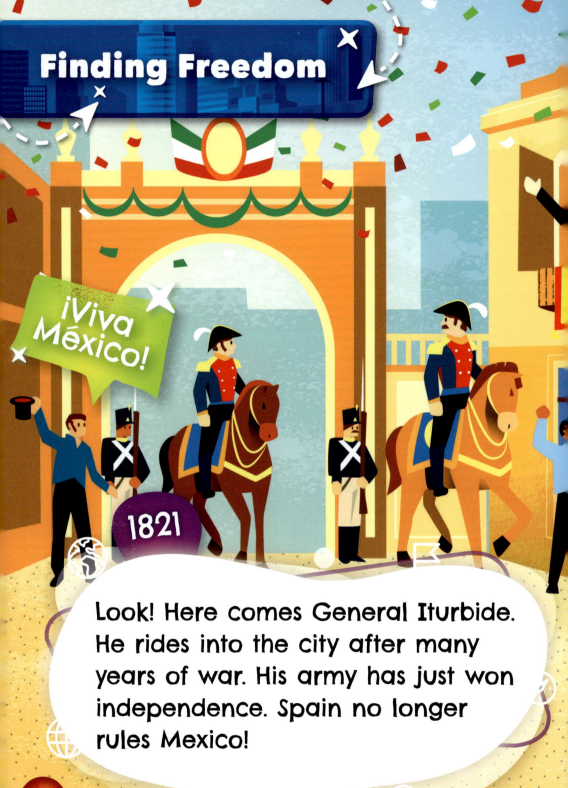

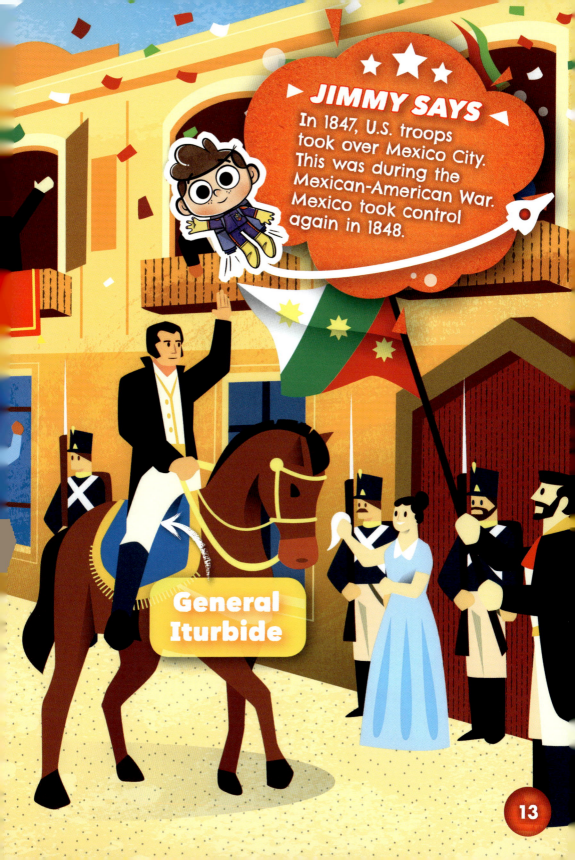

1929

The Mexican **Revolution** has shaken the country! The government wants to help its people come together.

It asked artists to create huge **murals** around the city. Here, Diego Rivera paints the history of Mexico!

Diego Rivera

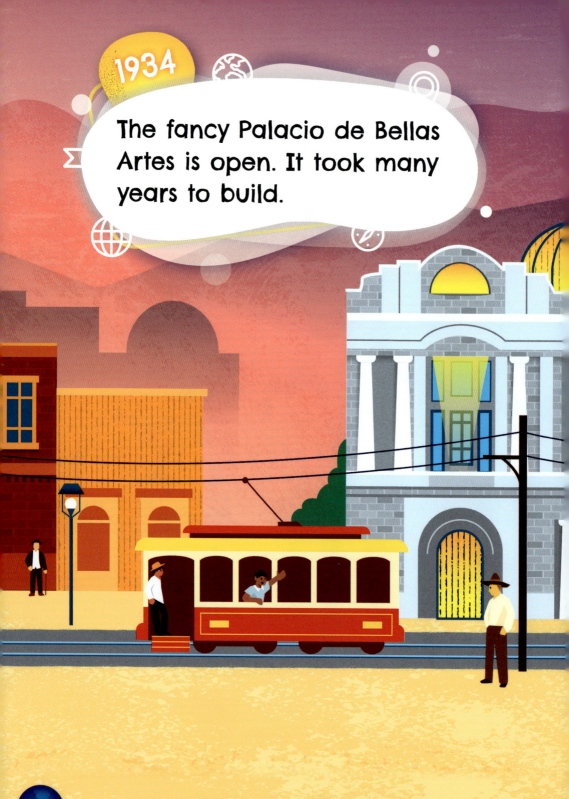

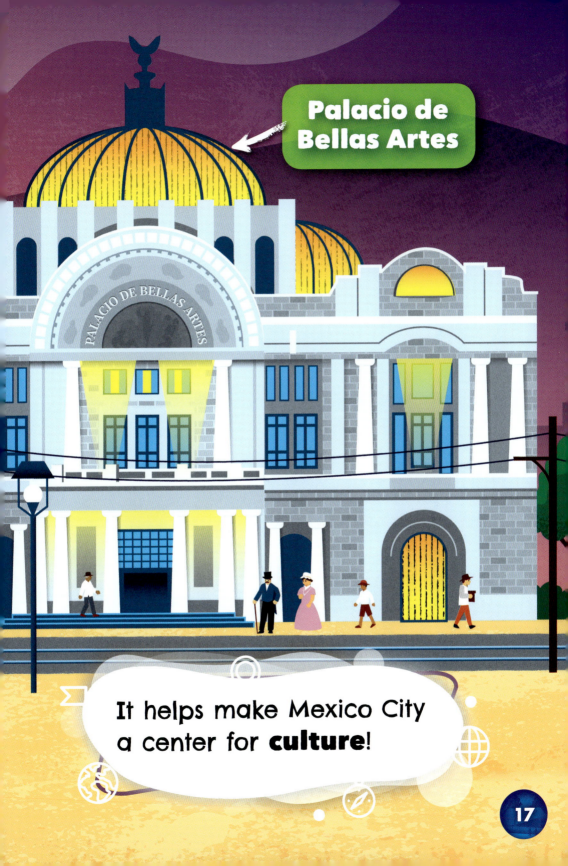

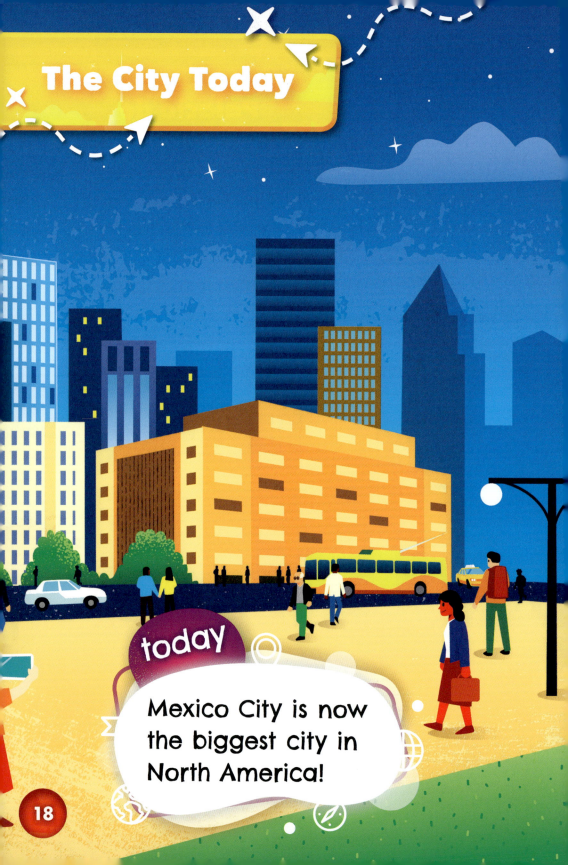

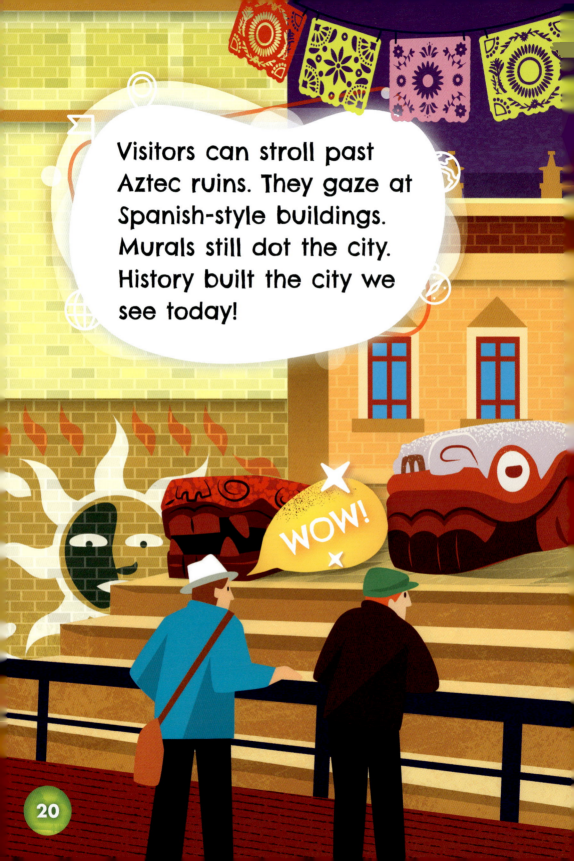

Mexico City Timeline

1325: The Aztecs found Tenochtitlán

early 1500s: Thousands of Aztec people live in Tenochtitlán

1521: The Spanish take over and destroy Tenochtitlán

1521 to early 1800s: The Spanish control the city

1821: Mexico wins independence from Spain

1910 to 1920: The Mexican Revolution causes battles throughout Mexico

1929: Diego Rivera paints the history of Mexico as part of a mural movement

1934: The Palacio de Bellas Artes opens

Mexico City, Mexico

Glossary

cathedral–the main Catholic church in an area

Catholics–people belonging to or relating to the Christian church that is led by the pope

culture–the beliefs, arts, and ways of life in a place or society

enslaved–to be considered property and forced to work for no pay

Indigenous–related to people originally from an area

mestizo–related to people who have mixed European and Indigenous backgrounds

murals–big works of art that are created on walls or ceilings

revolution–a sudden change in government

ruins–the remains of something that was destroyed

temples–buildings used for worship

To Learn More

AT THE LIBRARY

Dittmer, Lori. *Aztec Empire*. Mankato, Minn.: Creative Education, 2019.

Harmony, Cynthia. *Mi Ciudad Sings*. New York, N.Y.: Penguin Workshop, 2022.

Markovics, Joyce. *Mexico City*. New York, N.Y.: Bearport Publishing, 2018.

ON THE WEB

FACTSURFER

Factsurfer.com gives you a safe, fun way to find more information.

1. Go to www.factsurfer.com.

2. Enter "Mexico City" into the search box and click 🔍.

3. Select your book cover to see a list of related content.

BEYOND THE MISSION

> WHAT FACT FROM THE BOOK DID YOU THINK WAS THE MOST INTERESTING?

> WHERE IN MEXICO CITY CAN YOU SEE THE CITY'S HISTORY TODAY?

> DESIGN YOUR OWN ISLAND CITY. WHAT KIND OF BUILDINGS DOES IT HAVE? DRAW A PICTURE OF IT.

Aztec, 6, 7, 9, 11, 20
capital, 5, 6, 9
cathedral, 10, 11
Catholics, 10
Cortés, Hernán, 8, 9
founded, 7
independence, 12
Indigenous, 10
Iturbide, Agustín de (general), 12, 13
lake, 7, 10
mestizo, 10
Mexican Revolution, 14
Mexican-American War, 13
Mexico, 5, 12, 13, 14
murals, 14, 15, 20
North America, 18
Palacio de Bellas Artes, 16, 17
people, 6, 10, 14
Rivera, Diego, 14
ruins, 8, 9, 20
Spain, 9, 10, 12, 20
temples, 6, 7, 11
Tenochtitlán, 6
timeline, 21